Let's Go to Acadia National Park

Solve Problems Involving the Four Operations

Presley Adams

New York

Published in 2015 by The Rosen Publishing Group, Inc.
29 East 21st Street, New York, NY 10010

Book Design: Mickey Harmon

Photo Credits: Cover, p. 13 Zack Frank/Shutterstock.com; p. 5 Miro Vrlik Photography/Shutterstock.com; p. 7 John Greim/ Contributor/LightRocket/Getty Images; p. 9 Jeff Greenberg/Photolibrary/Getty Images; p. 11 Mark Daffey/Lonely Planet Images/Getty Images; p. 15 christab06/Shutterstock.com; p. 17 Piotr Krzeslak/Shutterstock.com; p. 19 Michal Ninger/ Shutterstock.com; p. 21 (garter snake) Gerald A. DeBoer/Shutterstock.com; p. 21 (four-toed salamander) Jason Patrick Ross/Shutterstock.com; p. 21 (frog) Ilias Strachinis/Shutterstock.com; p. 22 Denis Jr. Tangney/E+/Getty Images.

ISBN: 978-1-4777-4687-5
6-pack ISBN: 978-1-4777-4689-9

Manufactured in the United States of America

CPSIA Compliance Information: Batch #WS15RC: For further information contact Rosen Publishing, New York, New York at 1-800-237-9932.

Contents

A Family Trip

Every summer, my family takes a trip to Acadia National Park in Maine. I've learned a lot about the park after taking so many trips there.

Acadia National Park includes much of Mount Desert Island. The French were the first Europeans to land on the island on September 5, 1604. The island fell under British control in 1759 before becoming part of the United States after the Revolutionary War. In 1919, the area became the first national park east of the Mississippi River.

Acadia National Park was first called Lafayette National Park. The name was changed to Acadia in 1929 in honor of the name given to the land by early French **explorers**.

My family and I drive to Maine when we visit Acadia National Park. The **distance** from our house to the park is 800 miles. Our road trip takes 3 days. The first day, we drive 315 miles. The second day, we drive 321 miles. How many miles do we need to drive on the third day?

I can answer the question by setting up a math problem, or equation, with *m* standing for the unknown number of miles.

To make this equation easier to **solve**, I can break it into 2 steps. First, I add 315 and 321 to get 636. Then, I subtract 636 from the total number of miles we drive, which is 800. The answer is 164 miles.

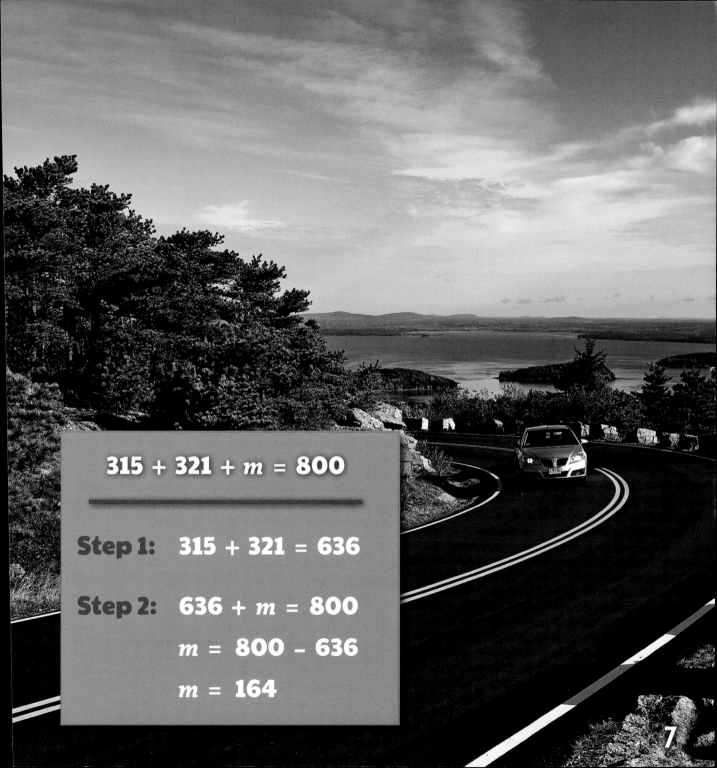

$$315 + 321 + m = 800$$

Step 1: $315 + 321 = 636$

Step 2: $636 + m = 800$

$m = 800 - 636$

$m = 164$

Take a Hike!

Acadia National Park is a great place to hike. My family and I hike together and always stay on the park's trails.

There's a lot of land for hiking in the park. It has 125 miles of trails. My family and I hike 3 miles a day for 3 days. How many miles of trails would be left for us to hike after those 3 days are done?

This question can be set up as another 2-step math problem. I use **parentheses** to show which part of the equation I'm going to do first. After multiplying 3 by 3 to make 9, I subtract 9 from the total number of miles. Subtracting 9 from 125 equals 116.

Order of Operations

parentheses > multiplication and division > addition and subtraction

$$(3 \times 3) + m = 125$$

Step 1: $3 \times 3 = 9$

Step 2: $9 + m = 125$

$m = 125 - 9$

$m = 116$

Carriage Roads

On our hikes, my family and I see the **carriage** roads that have been part of the park since the early 1900s. They were built so horses and carriages could travel through the park.

Signposts still stand at the corners of the carriage roads. These were used to direct carriage drivers. We count 72 signposts during our trip. My parents count signposts for 3 days, and I count signposts for another 3 days. We count an equal number each day. How many signposts did we count each day?

By breaking this problem into 2 steps, I can see that we count 12 signposts each day. There are 45 miles (72 km) of carriage roads at Acadia National Park. That means there are a lot of signposts to count!

$$72 \div (3 + 3) = s$$

Step 1: $3 + 3 = 6$

Step 2: $s = 72 \div 6$

$s = 12$

Beautiful Beaches

My family and I also like to walk along the beaches at Acadia National Park. This is a great way to see the Atlantic Ocean. Many of the beaches are rocky, but some are sandy.

I like to look at shells along the sandy beaches. I see 20 shells each day for 2 days. Some are broken, and some are whole. If 9 of the shells I see over those 2 days are broken, how many whole shells do I see?

To find the answer, I first multiply 20 by 2 to find the total number of shells I see (40).
Then, I subtract the 9 broken shells from 40.
I see 31 whole shells on the beaches.

$$(20 \times 2) - 9 = s$$

Step 1: $20 \times 2 = 40$

Step 2: $s = 40 - 9$

               $s = 31$

The ocean moves away from the shoreline during low tide. That's a good time to see animals in small tide pools. I like to see starfish. Their 5 arms make them look like stars.

I see 4 starfish 1 day and 3 starfish another day. How many starfish arms do I see altogether if each starfish has 5 arms? First, I add 4 and 3 to get 7 total starfish. Then, I multiply 7 by 5 arms to make 35 arms total.

There are over 40 miles (64 km) of shoreline to explore in Acadia National Park!

$$(4 + 3) \times 5 = a$$

Step 1: $4 + 3 = 7$

Step 2: $a = 7 \times 5$

$a = 35$

So Many Trees!

Acadia National Park has forests with a wide **variety** of trees. I see 535 total trees in an area of the park. They're spruce, maple, and oak trees. There are 105 oak trees and 92 maple trees. Each of these numbers is close to 100.

How many spruce trees are in that area? I can round the other numbers to the nearest 100 to help me find the answer in my head. I can see if the answer I get by rounding is close to the answer I get by solving the real equation.

Rounding is a good way to **estimate** and see if your answer is reasonable. You can round in your head because the numbers are easier to work with. Are the answers for the 2 equations close to one another? If they are, the answer is reasonable.

rounding

$$100 + 100 + s = 500$$

Step 1: $100 + 100 = 200$

Step 2: $200 + s = 500$

$$s = 500 - 200$$

$$s = 300$$

solving

$$105 + 92 + s = 535$$

Step 1: $105 + 92 = 197$

Step 2: $197 + s = 535$

$$s = 535 - 197$$

$$s = 338$$

Falcons in Flight

Many species, or kinds, of birds make their home in Acadia National Park. My favorite bird is the peregrine falcon. This large bird is a predator that can hunt other animals at speeds of up to 180 miles (290 km) per hour.

Young peregrine falcons stay with their parents until they learn to fly and hunt. It takes them around 35 days to grow wings big enough to fly. Then, it takes another 6 weeks for them to learn to hunt.

How many days do young peregrine falcons stay with their parents? First, I multiply the 6 weeks spent learning to hunt by 7 days per week, which equals 42 days. Then, I add 42 days to the 35 days it takes for their wings to grow. To check my answer, I round 42 and 35 to the nearest 10 to make the addition easier. Is my answer reasonable? Yes!

$$35 + (6 \times 7) = d$$

solving	rounding
Step 1: $6 \times 7 = 42$	**Step 1:** $6 \times 7 = 42 \triangleright 40$
Step 2: $d = 35 + 42$	**Step 2:** $35 \triangleright 40$
$d = 77$	$d = 40 + 40$
	$d = 80$

19

Amphibians and Reptiles

There are many other kinds of animals to see at Acadia National Park, too. Amphibians and reptiles are my favorite kinds of animals. I like to look for those while we hike through the park or visit its beaches. I see different species of frogs, snakes, and salamanders.

I see 64 frogs, snakes, and salamanders on our trip. If I see 25 frogs and 11 snakes, how many salamanders do I see? How would you solve this problem and use rounding to check your answer?

$$25 + 11 + s = 64$$

four-toed
salamander

bullfrog

garter snake

Protected Lands

I love visiting Acadia National Park with my family. I learn so much about nature and different species of plants and animals. It's important to have this piece of **protected** land for them to live and grow. It means someday I will be able to take my children to this park to see all the wildlife I love to look at now.

I want to visit other national parks, too. Have you ever visited a national park?

One of the coolest things to see at Acadia National Park is Cadillac Mountain. It reaches a height of 1,530 feet (466 m)!

Glossary

carriage (KEHR-ihj) A wheeled vehicle pulled by horses and meant to carry people.

distance (DIHS-tuhns) The space between two points.

estimate (EHS-tuh-mayt) To use math tools, such as rounding, to find an answer that is close, but not exact. Also, the answer you get.

explorer (ihk-SPLOHR-uhr) Someone who travels to find new places.

parentheses (puh-REHN-thuh-seez) A pair of rounded marks used to group parts of a math problem.

protect (pruh-TEHKT) To keep safe.

solve (SAHLV) To find an answer for.

variety (vuh-RY-uh-tee) A number or collection of different things.

Index